WINDOWS AND MIRRORS

A.J. Montesi

Windows and Mirrors

Cornerstone Press
St. Louis

Second Printing

First Printing
Copyright © 1977 by A.J. Montesi

Library of Congress Cataloging in Publication Data
Montesi, A.J.   Windows and Mirrors
I. Title
Catalog Card No.: 77-89821
ISBN 0-918476-00-3

Printed in the United States of America

For Aleco

Acknowledgment is made to the following publications for poems that have appeared in them:
Eads Bridge Review, *Laughing Man*, *Laughing*, *The Webster Review*, *WEID*, *Image*, and *The St. Louis Literary Supplement*

CONTENTS

Cover and Illustrations:
Michael Sinner

ONE

Memphis

"and the blind man on the corner sings
'The Beal Street Blues.' "
                         —W.C. Handy

"Propped upon my two knees,
I kissed a stone;
I lay stretched out in the dirt
And I cried tears down."
                         —W.B. Yeats

"Without art man might find his life
on earth unlivable."
                         —Fyodor Dostoevsky

Dream Visions of Aleco

Landscape #1

Around, around the only rip of
silence . . . the frayed air nibbling at
the edge of stillness . . . the wash of
half and no light . . . the unbearable
weight of nothingness

I.

There was a morning freshness about you, *Aleco*.
as if you had just come from some rain-swept, green-fresh
     valley,
even when we would meet in the muted light of an early
morning
          one of those mornings that belong to the night
          that winter keeps.
As if we two only existed in time.
I stood in awe a little of your enormous paw-like hand,
ursiformed almost, as it would shadow-box playfully my
head and chin,
and watched as you mixed your morning toddy of whisky,
     sugar, and water,
offering me, a lad of six, a little of your *checato.*

II.

Then,
          somewhat older,
               there was something wrong with my legs.
And almost wet with tenderness, you would move with me —
     my small body
wrapped in those great arms — towards your Model T to
     Dr. Rudner's.

This passed, the legs corrected themselves.
But I have yet to forget your holding me;
your massive body geared mightily to pour
 its
great strength into my pained legs . . .
sheltering me with your enormous black
 coat
. . . clutching me as if I were the most
 precious
item on the earth.

III.

And then we'd be off to cross the wide Mississippi to steal
watermelons on the Arkansas side,
crossing the river at Memphis over the single span of the old
 Harahan bridge . . .
and then the rows of rich green watermelons against the
 black loam,
and the admonition to hurry
before a burst of buckshot
close to us would send all scurrying to the little Ford.
Over again the bridge with its drop and water below
frightening your squealing but happy children.

IV.

I remember, Aleco, on a Sunday morning
when we scrambled to get ready for church,
five pairs of brushed and polished shoes
waited for us as we frantically tried to get ourselves
together. And on returning . . . a whopping hot breakfast,
all prepared by those enormous hands.

V.

How did it come about that you were the adult *par excellence*
with children? You who could never relate to grown-ups,
growing awkward or silent in their midst.
But you were always first with the young ones — teasing,
     mugging,
and scowling your way into their joys.
I can recall going with you as your sole companion, a six or
     eight-
year old tow-headed boy, during the "dry" twenties to some
     hideaway
Negro bar, buried in Black Town, in pursuit of your morning
     shots.
Or standing on the bluff side of the Mississippi, during the
     1927
spring floods, watching swirling angry waters
swallowing up the whole of Arkansas.

VI.

I remember, *Aleco,* when I or others were sick,
after the operation or crisis, along in a stark, impersonal
hospital room, where all had been forbidden to enter,
suddenly you were there. First always in your coming:
commanding in your presence,
lighting up the room,
scattering nurse and doctor,
dismissing utterly our loneliness and fears.

VII.

Your death had been final and outrageous
as a cancer ate tirelessly through your side.
You who had been such a bulk of a man, muscularly lean and
     large-boned,
it was all I could do to carry you to the john
without feeling the rub of your bar ribs against
my shoulder . . . you were 70 pounds when you died.

5

VIII.

And when you were biered, lying in the stuccoed cheapness
of a commercial mortuary,
and we all sat about, longing for you a chapel of trees
and clean earth,
suddenly, there was a sound from an unused side entrance.
There, outlined, a man stood with a woman upgathered in his
    arms.
Once in, their figures made clear, we watched as your
        beloved Vi,
determinedly up from a hospital bed,
stood out from her husband's arms,
and struggling towards you,
crying, "Daddy," "Daddy,"
collapsed to the floor at your side.

IX.

And yet to others, to that mass of Italian immigrants
who came, to of all place, the American South,
you were the ill-favored son of a peasant dago dynasty,
all of whom had climbed to great wealth and power
. . . except yourself.
They had fired you periodically from the petty jobs they fed
        you,
claiming that your endless bottles of beer
and your morning shots of booze
sullied their lily-pure businesses.
But you were horse racing against a sun-filled horizon,
how could they dampen your spirit or will?

X.

I have sought for you since in a hundred others,
catching glimpses now and then in my lovers and friends.
Scanning each new face carefully with expectation and
        desire:

6

spending long years with a few, believing from some dim
    promise
that the ideal of you as a person had survived.
But the search was futile,
the face and hand empty:
nothing permanent was retrieved.

O *Aleco, Aleco,*
to me still the finest man in time,
no rude pistol shot ever
will shoot down from my dreams
your fierce ride against the sky.

Sketch: Daguerrotype of Nonno

Observe
how starkly he sits before the
strange camera. Like those figures from
Madame Tussaud's or in the waxworks in
Barcelona. If you would but touch them,
they would spring out at you . . .
from whatever place in time or death
they've been.

I.

Yepp, a *contadino*
straight from the rocks and fields of Ancona;
there you sit, old *grandioso*, mugging and scowling
with those ever-smacking mustachios.
And say, what's on top?
Nonno, wherever did you get that 1890's hat?

Remember Times Square before autos?
There
was a great problem with manure. Take all
those phaetons and carriages with their
horses.
The manure piled up in such stacks that the
city could not control it

What in the hell were you people like —
striking all those wild poses and grimaces?
Were you simply in a gas most of the time from your *vino*
. . . is that why you would collect and sing in the street?
Or was leaving that good dago soil and coming straight to
those
gaunt frame houses of America too much for you?

8

On April 23, 1896, at Koster and Bial's
Music Hall, in New York, the first official
showing of a motion picture took place. The
first audience moved away frightened from
the trains and waves that came straight out
at them from the new curious screen.

Tell me, old peasant, what was it like being you?

What is a snapshot anyway, *Nonno*? I
merely see a man and behind him a
stark screen. But look how afraid you
look. You, that great bull of a wop,
braying and snorting. I have seen your like
among other nationals, but rarely in the ranks of
your *amici*.

Was it not because you were afraid of the language, the
    strange new land
and the people?

            Surely wars, as barbaric as they are,
            and migration to other lands are the most
            that has happened to folk so far. For some,
            there was not even these.

Nor can I balk at the spaghetti-gothic of your clothes and
    houses.
For I am now convinced that you and yours were hardly
    afraid of,
or untouched by, genuine, passionate life.
Surely your lives were far richer than mine.

I have seen your "paesan" thrashing and weeping in the
    arms of their fat wives
I remember Angelo whose *capelli* turned overnight from
    black to stark grey
when his son was slain by the police.

9

And *Zia* Josie who sang arias from all the Verdi operas
and did her little jigs
and whose gay laughter rang through that filthy
    neighborhood
where we lived.
And the gaudy weddings and funerals. Remember, *Nonno*,
how you drank and danced at the Fruella wedding?
How none, young or old, could keep up with you

> On May 5, 1920, two Italian anarchists
> Niccola Sacco and Bartolomeo Vanzetti,
> were arrested for two alleged murders
> in South Braintree, Mass. They were
> subsequently electrocuted for being, as
> Judge Webster Thayer called them,
>   "Dagoes,"
> "sons of bitches," and "anarchistic
>   bastards."

> And Billy Sunday sang, "Give 'em the juice.
> Burn them. We've had enough of foreign
> radicals."

In an effort to know the secrets of your life's vitality,
I have tried to retrace your goings as best I could:
I have walked with you through the turnstiles at Ellis Island,
seen your eyes in emigrees entering Heathrow from India,
felt the lice crawling upon you as you emerged from steerage,
even sought for you on the *Ponte Vecchio* in Genoa, where
    you
disembarked for Amerika, Amerika.

> Bootleg trade in the U.S. in violation
> of the Eighteenth Amendment and the
> Volstead Act, was estimated in 1926
> at $3,600,000,000.

10

I have searched the faces of those peasant women in Spain
    Greece
and near the Appian way,
garbed in their eternal black, as if in mourning for life, for
    some
key to your fine life-sense.
But it will not come. We have lost it.
They are all dying out, those peasant wops. Their sons and
    daughters
are papier-mache and paste.
What gave you your mountains of life?

Was it because you were fortunate enough to be poor and
challenged by it?
Or that your children, experiencing both ill and good times,
never suffered the glut of plenty?
Or was it that we have wandered too far from the soil, and
    you and yours
were never too far from it?
Or simply does life emerge pure only out of conflict and
    suffering?

> In the 1920's burning crosses were
> frequently found before the workman's
> parish church of St. Thomas in South
> Memphis, Tennessee. In an open field
> a Negro was once hanged so that the
> school children from the parish school
> could not neglect to see him in their
> passing.

Can you recall, old lover, how stained with sweat
you would crawl down from a scaffolding
and give us all a big hug and kiss in your blue overalls.
And if anyone threatened us, you'd loom over them with a
    great scowl.

Of course, all backed away: who would fight a Latin giant?
All feared you . . . even the cops, for you were a mean old
    dog, my Nonno.

                    With the arrival of radio, in an effort
                    to better Anglo-Italian relations, an
                    Italian Hour appeared on the local station.
                    The twins played the accordian, and Zia
                    Sofia sang, "Tre, sienta-tre."

And so
            there you stand before me in this black-and-white
                image:
            your eyes reaching out to warn and love me still.
            I see the huge fist of my age reaching in to stamp out
                your presence,
            but there are some that will not let it.

            And quiet after making love, I see them will their
                seed into the cells
                of a child who will be like you.
            We will get you again, old fox,
            and see your features well up again in our children.
            Rest well, the photograph still remains.

Tribute to Malya

I.

La vecchia snoops birrd-like in the long corridors
    Her
        crony the straw man in the broom.

In the mammoth nose and mouth of *il vecchio*, there are
    shards of loose refuse . . .

        Here are not prints of dewinged
        angels left adoor;
        only the stark, only the bland authority
        of a single red bulb that fronts my mother's door.

II.

(R — bedded wrongside out in a smaller and smaller cubicle;
    beside the
cotton gauze and catheter — you, my mother's cell mate.)

Good morning, Miss R.   */ What do you do, wretch?*

Your little blue eyes have   */ Are those your eyes, those slits*
a good clean look about them,   *of ebbing glints?*
dear Miss R.

The sunshine pours through   */ Is it you, R, behind that*
your windows. Do you remember   *rotting and*
your summer garden?   *corroding flesh?*

Look, dear Miss R, we   */ Here we see your arm*
bring you some yellow   *go; here your leg.*
tulips from the south beds.

Miss R, you are looking fine   */ Good god, R, don't you*
this morning. Your face has   *remember*
a nice color to it.   *what a great beauty you*
                                once were?

III.

the inmates of the Raleigh Institute
are rub-a-dub-dub. surely.
In their curvature of magnolias and azaleas,
in their opulent structure,
they lead exemplary old lives.

Here not lorgnetted *dame* passes air and cackles.
Here no couponed old gentleman rolls unnoticed spitballs
of his own excrementa.
Here one learns to die elegantly
at the price of $20.000 per anum.
Here the *droit de seigneur* reigns
in the *ancien regime* of the Raleigh Institute.

IV.

The approach to the nether room of Malya's is lined
with mucused shades who jig to walk.
Here one disheveled crone spit curses on her neighbor;
further on the landing an old gent falls squarely on his face;
there a little woman weeps soundlessly all the day.
Observe the little lady in the corner.
Her hair is neatly combed;
her dark dress is freshly ironed;
her face and eyes appear serene;
she has just stopped two oldsters from quarreling.
See how she dispenses order and tenderness.
Look how they gather about her.

V.

Listen, little Malya, to my own dying day, I will not
forget this triumph of your lasting grace
— lovely and kind and still genuinely beautiful;
your skin still a dazzling health —
your majestic small head beating against and defeating
all that grime and death.

14

TWO

The Ruhr Valley

Es irrt der Mensch, so lang er strebt.
—J.W. Von Goethe

"He was a poet and hated the approximate."
—Rainer Maria Rilke

The Sisters of Mercy of Essen

As if
concrete + mortar + coal — much, much coal — coal
so pervasive
that *die leute* had to tunnel through it to underpass
the Ruhr.

As if
this could block out in some octopod manner the
responses that the
folk have always made to natural order:

the forests, their green militarily uniform,
the tulips and rhododendrum forever at clipped
attention
the manicured lawns and shrubs standing at
rigid half mast
intact, their aesthetic and mathematics of
horticulture.

But by degrees,
the precision fades, melts into
the bacilli of cement;
its tubercules spreading into conic sections of
edifices — long, rumpish, stub-like — so
blatantly
ugly that they might have come from Gary or
Newark
or East St. Louis.

and yet there are echoes from the past.
Amidst the box-like protuberances, the
bulgingly fat Krupp factories, and the lines,
upon lines, upon
lines of clavate *autobahns*

there stands in a sad little corner of the town
untouched by bombs,
the cemented walled section of the whores,
    where
not one tree,

        not one single flower
        not one shrub is allowed to
          stand.

On this spring overcast Sunday
those dumpty curled-up cumuli of the Ruhr
were again massing together for rain.

    On Stahlstrasse, in the brothel section of
      Essen town, the women —
    their limbs coquettishly coiled,
    their undersides thrust forward,
    their orifices pulled outward in the old
      stances of the Nile or Tiber,
    as if their openings were the center of the
      entire world —
    were gathering on one side of the narrow
      street.

They exhibited, flaunted, teased and tempted, displaying ass,
thigh, or breast to whoever might be ogling them there.
    Their eyes all the while staring or darting or drifting
    to the lonely men who walked singly or in pairs
      across
    the one street that bisected the tiny section.

    But the lonely men of Essen, *gastarbeiten* among
      them,
    walking, turning, turning, walking; forever
      watching —
    set up a similar charade: not of attraction but of
      neglect.

For as the promenade continued and continued (the
       prey caught
naked in the naked eye) not one male crossed the
       narrow
cobbled street.

With lazy coquetry,
               culled from hundreds of years of
                  experience
               the women kept to their preening and
                  striking of poses.
               One beautiful tall black begins again to
                  strut and glide.
               One Eurasian. unopened as the bud of
                  some exotic flower.
               flipped her slim behind. and a gold
                  fraulein. light as
               some sun ray.
               began to rub her lovely breasts,
               but still no male crossed the narrow line.

One thought of the bustling whores of Amsterdam. of the
       poules of Pigalle
of the New Orleans hustlers. of the matron-like professionals
of *Wien*.

. . .

       But the women, their manikin struts unheeded. were
          already gathering
       in threads of yawning lines.

But driving on, we were immediately attracted to a stud-pimp
       in his
opulent Alfa-Romeo, flanked by his hen whores. all richly
       dressed, all
fluttering around their rooster-daddy.

20

II.

Later, however, we drove further still into Essen
and came inevitably to the small "house" museum, carefully
tended and guarded, where the first Krupp had fired his
first piece of superior steel, and by degrees built the
first totally industrial city of *Deutschland*.

And looking back at the uncrossed street of
Stahlstrasse,
the disease of concrete, of young Essen
emerging alongside ancient Roman Koln,
the Krupp factories and the museum,
the lonely men and their untouched whores
came to us as a finally rounded circle.

And looking ourselves ahead, looking further and
further into the lonely future mornings of the
cement and steel capital of the district, Essen,
konig city of the Ruhr,
we thought we saw some webbed and scaly creature,
Piltdownishly ugly, finally pulling down the
cement walls that enclose the brothel section
of Stahlstrasse.

Der Dom zu Munster

Pfingsten 1975

With tracery and fluting conmingling Roman and Gothic
meanderings . . .
here a fitful buttress, here a rounded arch, and mulberry
windows, windows, windows — mullioned, recessed, and one
      gigantically rosed,
the majestic structure rises, rises . . .
at first struggling with ascent,
but once free of its middle girding,
drives beyond its earth-bound trajectory
and refining now the reluctant air
paces with the sun.

And within, free fall, space converging to some new
      otherness:
one's legs buckles, grappling to stay afloat.
And hands . . . smoothed to an ancient flatness,
suddenly become other
and almost relax into a prayer.
And by degrees, some presence — distant at first,
      but nearing,
becoming at last distinct, palpable, almost sentient —
gathers in some solemn procession
to the central altar
where it becomes unbelievably still.
And stepping, I step upon
and treading, I climb upon
the backs of a hundred million dead,
whose orisioned energy I have lived upon,
whose past pain has put me into time
and I am dumb with sonhood.

The nerves and cells transmuted
by some touch of ambient grace,
one paces now the labyrinth of the place:
until turns and side altars bring him to
an enormous fan-shaped clock, so gigantic in its workings,
    so splendidly
crafted in its red wood, that one glides almost unwittingly
    to its sounds,
moving out with its tempos to some vast cosmic ground,
timeless and eternal in its round.
One passes gradually on to a chapel. radiant with candles.
    where richly
garbed clerics. their voices lambent and plangent, sing out
    their grave *kyries.*
While before them, a magnificent tabernacle of the most
    brilliant silver,
blacksmithed by distant angels, reflects their infinite care.
And finally one reaches the cynosure of the *dom:*
a giant Saint Christopher, *doloroso*, grimacing in his pain,
    looming out from
a great pillar, his hand clutching a giant staff, his great back
    carrying
the tiny child.

II

But once the great edifice lay shattered.
In its entrance are mounted photographs that detail
the crumbling naves and columns, the gutted walls, the
    splattered altars.
The target of endless Allied bombs, at war's end it lay
    hopelessly doomed.
But, then, step by painstaking step, its reconstruction began.
As if urged by some wondrous devotion, some immense
    prayer, the people of
Munster fitted stone, wood, and metal into their old
    symmetries.

And by degrees chancel and altar, nave and pilaster rose
    to their old
heights
and one sun-drenched day, the cathedral once more lived.

And so at *Pfingsten zeit, Mai, 1975, I an auslander*, am moved
to stone-center.
I am become agatized, myself a part of the aggregate
    masonry that towers
before me.
Here men have acted admirably for once:
cross-patching some little light for all that darkness.
Starkly, another still looms in the foyer's picture gallery:
a plaque which contains a remnant stone from the cathedral
    at Coventry,
itself blasted and destroyed by another armada during
    the war.
And the plaque reads, "Let us forgive each other for these
    shared atrocities."
And each summer in the underbasement at Coventry, the
    Jugend of Deutschland
have spent much of their holiday helping to restore the church
that their *Luftwaffe* fathers had razed to nothing.
"Let us forgive each other as Christ forgave us," the plaque
    concludes.

Afterwards, outside on the Domplatz, returning to the self
    that the other
self denies:
I have become unnamed.
I thought of men in space ships hunting space for another of
    their kind,
of men starving to death in India while surrounded by cattle.
But my experience was too awesome to be denied, and
    looking at the faces
that passed before me
suddenly I too saw, I too was quickened, I too hoped
    once again.

Der Dom zu Munster (German translation by Robert Drysdale)

Pfingsten 1975

Durch Masswerk und Riefen laufen romanische und
    gotische Meander
ineinander uber . . .
hier ein aufbrechender Strebepfeiler, hier ein Rundbogen.
    und weinrote
Fenster, Fenster, Fenster — abgeteilt, zuruckgetreten
    und eins
grossartig rosettenhaft,
die majestatische Struktur strebt aufwarts, aufwarts
zunachst sich nach oben kampfend
einmal die mittleren Umgurtungen uberwunden
treibt sie aus ihrer erdgebundenen Umlaufbahn hinaus
und jetzt die widerstrebende Luft verfeinernd
schreitet sie mit der Sonne.

Und innen drin werden an Niete, Rad und Schlussel
    angeglichene
Hande und Knochel plotzlich uralt
und sinken fast in ein Gebet zuruck.
Und stufenweise wird man von Wellen umwogen,
Erscheinungen — zunachst weit entfernt, dann deutlicher
    werdend,
greifbar, furchtbar echt — die sich in einer feierlichen
    Prozession
zum Hauptaltar versammeln, wo sie fast unglaublich
    still werden.
Und schreitend, schreite ich auf
und tretend, trete ich auf
die Rucken von Hundert Millionen Toten
von deren Andachtselan ich gelebt habe,
deren vergangenes Leid mich in die Zeit gesetzt hat.
Hier habe ich vollkommenen Geist beruhrt
und ich bin stum vor Sohnschaft.

Die Nerven und Zellen von irgendeiner
Schopfung hochster Anmut verwandelt.
durchschreitet man nun das Labyrinth der Statte:
bis man durch Wendungen und Seitenaltare zu einer
grossartigen facherformigen Uhr gebracht wird, so
    uberwaltigend in ihre
Arbeitsweise, in ihrem roten Holz so wunderbar gefertigt,
   dass man zu
ihren Gerauschen fast ohne Wahrnehmung dahingleitet, mit
    ihren Tempi
hinausstrebend in irgendeine unfassbare kosmische Weite,
in ibrer Runde zeitlos und ewig.
Allmahlich gelangt man zu einer Kappelle, mit Kerzen
    ausgestrahlt, wo
gut gekleidete Kleriker mit sanften, schallenden Stimmen ihre
feierlichen Kyries erschallen lassen.
Wahrend vor ihnen ein grossartiger Tabernakel aus aufs
    Schonste
schimmerndem Silber, von weit entfernten Engeln
    geschmiedet, die
unendliche Anmut widerspiegelt.
Und schliesslich erreicht man den Mittelpunkt des Domes:
einen riesenhaften Heiligen Christophorus, doloroso, .
    dessen Gesich
sich in Schmerz verzieht, der aufstrebt von einem
    grossen Pfeiler,
seine Hand umgreift einen riesigen Stab, sein grosser
    Rucken tragt
das winzige Kind.

II.

Doch einst lag der grosse Dom tot da.
Am Eingang findet man Fotographien, die von der
    Zerstorung erzahlen;
sie zeigen ein Skelett zertrummerter Mittelschiffe und
    Pfeile; die

grossen Mauer ausgebrannt, die Altare ein
        Trummerhaufen. Von
Alliiertenflugzeugen zerschellt und ausgebombt, lag er
        hoffnungsles tot.
Aber dann ein muhevoller Schritt nach dem anderen bauten
        seine Leute
wieder auf. Und wie durch irgendeine wunderbare
        Hingebung gezwungen, ein
inniges Gebet, setzten seine Wiederbauer Steine, Holz
        und Backsteine
in ihre alten Symmetrien ein und allmahlich gewannen
        Kanzel und
Altar, Mittelschiff und Pilaster ihre Standorte wieder und
eines hellen Tages lebte die grosse Kathedrale wieder.

Also bin ich, ein Auslander, um Pfingsten, Mai 1975,
        zutiefst geruhrt;
Ich werde in Achat verwandelt, werde selbst ein
        Bestandteil des
gesamten Mauerwerks, das vor mir aufragt.
Hier hat der Mensch ausnahmsweise vortrefflich
        gehandelt —
er hat den ganzen Schutt in Schoenheit verwandelt,
        die ganze fruhere
Hasslichkeit in Licht.
Neben den Fotographien steht kahl noch ein Mahnzeichen,
eine Plakette, die einen ubriggebliebenen Stein aus dem
        Dom zu
Coventry enthalt, der von den selben Kraften vernichtet
        und zertrummert
wurde, die Kirche zu Munster gefallt hatten.
Und auf der Plakette steht: "Vergebt einander diese geteilten
Greueltaten."
Und jeden Sommer verbrachte die Jugend Deutschlands im
        Unterkeller zu
Coventry einen grossen Teil ihrer Ferien damit, die
        Struktur zu

restaurieren, die ihre Vater der Luftwaffe dem
     Erdboden gleichgemacht
hatten.
"Vergebt einander, wie auch Gott euch vergeben hat," steht
am Schluss.

Nachher, auf dem Domplatz, zu meinem Selbst
     zuruckkehrend, das
das andere Selbst verleugnet,
stand ich da namenlos.
Doch war das Erlebnis zu ehrfurchtig. um es zu verleugnen,
     und als ich
in die Gesichter sah, die an mir vorbeigingen . . . plotzlich
     sah auch ich,
ging auch ich schneller, hatte auch ich wieder Hoffnung.

Hans

Laser beam Hans
slicing the air with your shouts and curses.
your long, stretched-out hands
reaching to the Bochum roof tops,
Largely walking, largely talking,
your huge bulk towering over the mastadon concrete.
Puffing, gesticulating wildly, your mind a switch yard
of counter signals.
It is hard side-stepping
the Prussian solider that stalks within you.

And yet, looking under and over one
finally comes to the wee man that you carry in your pocket.
He does not pace and turn, pace and turn.
Rather he keeps several objects in the air.
this pint-sized tumbler:
two swiftly bouncing reds, and a badly damaged old
        white ball.

Once you drove me to your Ruhr home,
past Moers, past Essen, past Dortmund
— driving furiously, talking wildly of rock music, Marx, and
        Plato.
But when we arrived at the small apartment house
your neighbors smirked and sniggered at your coming:
and no father met us at the door with a frown.
nor did mother or brother sit with us
at stiff attention
during our solemn, laughless meal.

Manfred

Gentle, patient Manfred,
infinitely soft and lyrical,
with his matted hair and long beard,
believing solemnly in Marx's Cinderella romance with the
    worker,
wearing his jeans with almost soldier-like fidelity.
There is, however, no saber-rattling or bush-skirmishing
in his young heart.
He's a nineteenth century old-fashioned bourgeois boy,
a Tonio Kroger or a Demian.
Even his beard, scrupulously scrubbed and combed,
reminds one of the beard that brushed Freud's face
when he himself was young in Vienna
and himself young alone.

Bettina

Bettina, Bettina
with your sharply mascared eyes
and boots
— blackly leathered —
snaking up your buns and thighs.
You're a Berlin girl, a Dusseldorf swell,
not a big-boned women from the Ruhr.

In your black ballooning skirts and tooled-leather shirts.
leaving classes abruptly for Rhodes, Istanbul. Athens . . .
with all sorts of young men
— straight mostly, but others kinky with just a touch or two of
    deSade —
and the slow return, without prelude or ceremony. your
    lovers
tossed aside as rapidly as those endless gold-tipped
    cigarettes —
your young beautiful head bent solemnly at your desk
buried in the poetry of Yeats.

There is not, you claim, sitting in the glow of a new sun tan
    during
one of those grim Ruhr winters, enough air and sunshine.
    enough booze and sex,
in the whole wide world for you;
and that life's every moment should be intense,
lived to the very marrow of the bone.
"Bettina, Bettina," we'd howl, "You're not real. a nineteenth
    century chick,
perhaps. but not a real "now" person."

But I remember the nights when we would all go to your
    favorite bar
and your presence and laughter were so infectious
that every man in the place wanted to make love to you

hoping to touch somewhere in your body
that rich source of life that you hold.
But I would watch your eyes looking always beyond them,
always at the door, always at the vacant chair.

It, then, did not much surprise me
after I had long left the Ruhr Valley
When they told me you had died
caught between an axle and a rod
on an autobahn leading into Munich.

Gretchen

*a tall knee
and a backside, thin and boney
no breasts at all.*

At scatter,
the twos and digits push and clamor
their thin legs dart through eyeballs and hair
x's and y's conmingle
not touch the tough geometric stars.

The shouts ride and drop:
fill the playing field with back and front dirty
words, kind dirty words,
"Nein, gut, nicht,"
The head-butted ball falls to the rag-tail grass.

But Gretchen
is not a mouth-chopping intellectual
overtalking all,
seeing nothing.
She is not introspective, reflective;
she's a life person,
an earth one.

There are no pastels or soft shades here, you insist. Only dark
monochromes — a land of foghorns, not a nuance in an acre.
            (Read as one line, two voices)
The mystery of chemistry and electricity */ But ineradicable
                                              is my memory*

yoked to a formula of ions and —   */ those legs . . .
                                              they were all
                                              float and*

if you would but touch this fabric   *rubber. She
                                              would collapse*

33

a mild shock would go rolling through

you. The life nearest is a whip not
a toad.

Magnificent spirit — like a filly

that they overbred in Kentucky

until in a race those denaturized

legs flew apart. She balances out

a hundred suicides. "Not so,
perhaps an exquisite eccentric
— slightly but sensitively mad."

/ *even in those*
  student
  recitals . . .

/ *blacking out —*
  falling off the
  piano
/ *stool after her*
  flourishes and
  diminuendoes.
/ *her listeners*
  were frozen as
  they watched
/ *a kind of polio . . .*
  some defect of
  the
/ *bone or blood.*

Yet even when crawling or floored,
fighting tenaciously to rise: she was tough,
the beads of sweat breaking out on her old face.
And if someone would hurry to help,
she'd pop them with that cane.

Why did she return there?
Her father was an arch enemy of Hitler,
and was sent out in exile during the '30's.
And she was forbidden as a child to attend school
in Deutschland.
She left for England.

The trees are of some fine porcelain or glass;
they seem arranged
as items in a surgical dressing
an order of white military exactitude.

(Many years later after the fall of the Third Reich
and the death of her husband, Gretchen returned to Germany
to music at a newly constructed university
in a district where the kaisers
had forbidden any university at all.
"The Ruhr people," they had ordered, "will remain
    the drones
of Germany.")

Gretchen knew few rules or commandments:
except the ones that were important.
she lived with her students
in cracker-box dormitories
in communal apartments,
in old crumbling farm houses.
Followed only by her one upright piano.
Counseling, tutoring
surrounded by her innumerable followers:
her children of all ages and sizes.

I remember one day going to her place for a language lesson.
One little chap, tow-headed and earnest, about eight,
    was trying
to teach me the German umlauts.
His little face would light up when he corrected
    my bad German.
"I must save them from their Wilhelm and Hitler past,
and from their parents,
who do not teach love but stoic acceptance."
Gretchen would say to me.
"See how fine they are, my lads and lasses."
And when I turned to nod agreement,
Gretchen had already fallen to her face
as her thin legs buckled.
And we again watched as she struggled to get up.
Then it was done; she stood upright, and turning cheerfully
    said to me,
"Now, we shall go on with your lesson."

THREE

St. Louis

"Ripeness is all: the rest is silence.
Love is all; we are such stuff as love
has made us . . ."
                    —Delmore Schwartz

"It was a madness to look down
On the toy city where
the glittering mentality of
clock and chocolate . . .
Made every morning somewhat
Less than you coud bear."
                    —James Merrill

"Think where man's glory most begins and ends,
And say my glory was I had such friends."
                    —W.B. Yeats

Poem

This is not a killer poem.
It does not mean to strangle me or
to throw me roughly to
the ground;
or attempt to knife, shoot, or poison
me with its thin hands.
Nor is it a "Dream" poem or a "Daddy" poem
or even a "Bells" poem.
If it is not a love poem,
it's at least a friendly one.
Look, I have even managed to get one
affectionate arm half way around its slack shoulder.

Finis

the tears you are shedding
        are black
                black of ink.
they run
       torpor
            like the flat-ending close of a whine
            like the slip-thread note of a sigh.

                 Stepping back,
                    circling,
                         I finally fist out:
                 but there is nothing to hit.

                 I cannot reach you in all of that film and
                     ink.
                 You are a mosaic of all those same voices,
                 all those tired lines
                 all those cliches that you disavow.

If I scratch through barely,
there are sticks and bits of paper
and all that glue . . .
                 I flay my arms,
                     "You're a non-person, a not-you.
                     How can I reason with a cluster of
                        bromides?"

I shout and gesture wildly
I storm and sputter;
and then in a step, circling,
I meet myself in the round
             and listening,
                      hearing my own sounds,
                 I suddenly realize I have formed the very
                     same lines, I

        look down
                My arms are a long stick.
        Looking at my thigh,
                        I see the self-same wires.

And your tears
                black
                        black of ink
                                drip everywhere upon me
                                until I wade thickly, slowly in the muck
                                that flows from you.

Until we have become two figures disappearing from the very
        same,
pale white, old old page.

Purna

the thrust of your back is generally
                              downward
your arms
              and
                    legs
                        pin the floor.
I want you to come towards me
                              slowly.
De-line your soles,
                    move outwardly.
Re-stretch your hands
                        your toes.
The frame before your eyes
                              must tilt
                                    turn
                                        upend.

See the spread of light before you:
                              it is neither linear nor
                                    circular.

DO YOU THINK YOU CAN REACH IT?

Now,
          are you moving out
                              are you moving out
are you moving out
                    of time
                              of western time
                                        out of the old
                                                    old
                                                          tem

Are you losing your old balances?
Are you ensheathed in a new wave of light?

****

Are you coming to our *ashram*?
Are you coming to Auroville?
Are you finding the Mother, the new Divine Mother?
Are you attaining purna, peace; purna, peace;
purna, peace.

Lines to Theodore Dreiser

Old wily codger with your squinting bad eye,
decked out in your purple shirts and yellow ties,
you're still the mayor or Chico
still our honorable duce.
Your sons have worsted all the pale owners.
They learned fast that a job is taken with a fist,
and that several fists give even a mick or a dago status.
See, your sons fill the public chambers:
judges, governors, mayors, presidents . .
You taught us the age's economics:
America's streets were lined with guns and gold.

Surely that was not Sister Carrie I saw this morning;
she was behind the wheel of a shining new Cadillac . .
Why only last month I saw her on Maxwell street
admiring a cheap dress in a store window.
And Drouet is still very much with us;
he still quotes all the ball scores of the weekend,
still knows all the latest jokes
and grows red in the face talking about
the success of his corset sales.

Yet, take heart, beautiful old man, weeping the
        streets of Chicago
at the spectacle of the ghetto poor walking before you.
Did you know that your grandsons are at last appearing
        among us.
See, they are returning to those old shacks
near the railroad trestles,
and go out with you each moring
to pick up pieces of discarded coal
in those first cold dawns of America's early century,
whose rich promise America neither met nor kept.
Look how these young poor are so rich,
for all your Clyde Griffiths lie dead.

For the Wedding of the Painter Sebastian
   and His Mary

I

You two come twain in this sweet hour
when your young dreams float about you
as some gold-spun web that nets out dark and shadow.
At this gallant hour, we enter momently your garden
and mark how like Saint Sebastian of the arrows,
writhing in exquisite pain,
does appear our own Sebastian, whose hands have oft
      wrought
beauty out of pain's despite.
And our gentle Mary, like all the Marys of old,
does diffuse in her serene movements,
in her radiant gift for life,
a promise that only a zion could bear.
What thrust of loin or heart,
what foot, what climb on the sleep-locked avenues
of mind
could catch
the emerald light that plays upon you,
the new green leaves, the fresh nosegays that rest
upon your eyes and hair.

II.

Although moved and heartened by your love, some ask,
"What manner of creatures are these
who have dared to enter this old garden
who have quickened it with such fresh new blossoms?"
. . . Do they not know
that the waters of the mind are dark and secret.
They hold to no constancies; they cup their sails to no winds
      of
past or future consistencies.
They fail or flaw all that men will, all that men hope.
Surely, their garden will sink.

45

III.

Do not fear, my gamin lovers, your garden will not die.
Have I not seen in all your pain and strugglings,
in the agonies of your strivings,
glimpses of new worlds, new horizons.
Have I not seen you wrest
from the ills of a pained and tormented age
the fierce will to love the poor world
despite its ugly flounderings.
Out of your gift to make beauty
out of your will to affirm love,
Lo, your garden quickens:
                            its seeds already kiss the light.

Wedding Lines for Tom and Linda

On this sun-flooded day,
           the light gathering about you
we are become all visual.
           Our eyes glance from head to heart
           from boot to belt
           and knead with your fingers
           their distraught path.

Yet despite the moment's weight,
you move into promise.
And for that we would not wish for you too easy of a future —
one blocked out of every dayness,
draining out to a vegetable dullness.

           Nor could we wish for you a fuss of troubles,
           tonic and bracing as they might be.
           For although too much trial would make
           life taut as a drawn bow,
           it would not spare your wholeness.

Nor do we sigh for you
too hot a passion, too much of ardor; for too great an
intensity soon cools to an icy nothingness. The geography of
    the
mind bends less to excesses; its lines crisscross from order to
    order.

But on this luminous day,
we do hope for you a union so peppered with creativity
that its cry will spill out to the great world.
For this poor globe needs much the cleanly shaped
logic of your will and the quiet strength of your newly joined
    hands.
For they in creeping one into the other have already stopped
    their
turbulent career,
and have become as one in some new rich harmony.

May these joined hands reach further and further
into our dark corners and illuminate them with their air
And may they — in their repose and generosity —
remained crossed all the days of your future years.

Menorca, Summer, 1974

Street Muse

They've got you by the throat, woman!
Got you carrying stolen loot between your thighs for
your stud man.
Can't you see if you don't behave,
you'll lose all respectability?
Don't you realize with your cheap, knotted-at-the top
net hose, high heels, and faked Marie Antoinette wig,
you've been too busy hustling the wrong side of the road?
They are talking about "silence" now and something
other than a page.

We liked you far better when you fluttered your brocaded
fan in salons or drawing rooms,
where you would airily babble "O Art, O life,"
but you're not welcome in these places any longer,
you've been hanging around the streets and pavements too
    long.

Stop that crying, woman.
All is not finished.
Your gang waits around still,
and although they're not talking of *fin du race*
or *fin du siecle*.
when they lift their red mouths to speak
nothing, nothing comes out,
except the thin pule that you picked up on the streets.
Better reform, woman,
before it's too late.

Memorial Lines for Orion

The age broke into little pieces:
its ventricles and canals blurring,
the red spouting from drains and sewers,
the wash blotting out the plains and rivers.

Caught in midstride,
your shanks already coiled to that
fiercely taut ballet,
you refused to see the awful form
that flopped and convulsed before you,
and flung those wondrous fingers
to the skies.

With flywheel touch
and rivet hand,
you carved and sculptured where you could
— transmuting all that darkness into light,
for to you all ugliness was but clay to beauty,
all sickness but a prelude to health.

Then step by exacting step
your form bent to some magnificent
precision in the dark,
we watched that amazing acrobatic
that translated dirt into grace, muck into light,
and mire into a prodigious beauty. . .
Where once stood snags and brambles,
shale and grime,
there grew a wonder of greenery
and stark within this garden's center
a tower that
shot its way to the sun.
Even brutal Joliet bent to your heart's metaphor.

But look.
impaled upon that tower is the
suffering man we would not see.
Filled with his own energy of self-doubt and weakness,
carrying the full sting of the time's devils.
he wrestles with the mask he knows that he must wear.

Until one quick day,
his work spilled out before him.
we saw him topple,
his hands still describing
those arcs — defining, collecting, reaching.

But then the roaring air.
its ripples coasting wildly about us
uplifted his yet flailing body
until that mighty heart lay still.

Some moved without their knowing;
they crawled out of hole and cellar;
they stumbled to the Joliet dwellings;
they reached for the old tools and gear.
Faces uplifted, eyes pointed,
sounds stifled deep within them,
they await the old directives.
But the studio is empty, the rooms, silent,
for our beloved Orion lies dead.

Blessed Black, what was your race or name?
Through your pair of eyes, all things were sacramental
— the earth you molded
      the men and women you loved
        the woods and animals of The Hill —
Provide, provide your grace and will
until upon every man's tongue will dance
those holy hosts of art and love
that you gave your life to sun.

The Death of Literature

Onside, his legs batting furiously,
the helmeted figure rose and fell,
rose and fell,
until form and cycle blurred to a sharp oneness.
as at once the giant Harley
spattering the grit and sand
swiveled to an awkward stillness.

Degoggled, the helmet now askew.
the spouted nozzle munching the dreaded air.
Orbs, slit-soft, turning from the awful sun.
its limbs circling the cylindered stock.
the cyclist passes air and bends finally to
the azoth block.

Half-boots turned inward, matted hair and beard buckling
fiercely in the mindless wind, the rider
surgeons the crippled wheel.
But the tour is useless, the wrench inadequate:
the Harley neither stirs nor "sputs."
The rider spits his last wad of chew
and slumping to the damp ground
slumbers, snoring with an awful sound.

At last, the cyclist stands at loss upright
and catching momently the last rays of light
surveys Bogartly the on-coming night.
When as though unleashed from nowhere
there appears
bounding furiously upon the treacherous strand
a giant mastiff hound
and hurling himself upon the standing man
flings him upon the fungoid sand.

Now upturned, lying in a maze of delighted fright,
the spit pushing through the tightened mouth,
the rider stares erotically into the crazed light
where dark and fur so overlie
that man appears dog
and dog, man.

At once teeth sink into the black leathered
and chain-decored thigh
a thin yell of pleasure
pounds the buttermilk sky.

In sweet recoil, the flesh hugging fully the jabs of pain
the cyclist stumbles for a random wrench
and in some amorous duet pitching himself against the bike
startles its engine back into life.

Struggling desirously, arms and legs tingling.
the bleeding driver recovers the roaring bike
and now mounted, pointing lovingly in the sheath of light,
he rears the Harley-Davidson at the panting hound.
But as if guided by wires, its body lashing sexually
the canine neither slows nor stops.

And there in some dumb-show relief,
the dog and bike thus engage
in a love-battle of fur and steel
until finally the canine lies disemboweled.
its entrails a rose of blood on the enamored wheels.

The Harley coughs once more,
and quietly, flatly stops its roar.
And altering once again to its scarecrow stance
assumes its position as before.

and nightward the scene discloses
the dead dog and the machine
entangled in some stark tableau

the man staring, staring minutes on
at the dead engine and the dog.
While overhead the moon,
daring not to disturb the scene
drifts behind a winter scroll
of dirty and discolored clouds.

(While slightly to the left, a putteed and bull-horned director
shouting, "Cut," disassembles the dead tableau. While an
exhausted camera crew reaches happily for the cold beer.
One spits.)

For Ethel

Dearest summer lady,
                loaded with the earth's plenties
                — squashes and melons, tomatoes and
                corn —

you ascend upon us
dispensing your greens with lavish hand,
                drawing us from our thin, lean lives
                to your rich loam and rain.
Out of what secret shade do you come?
    dispensing kindness and gentleness in a world
    in which the kind and gentle seem dying.
Your generosity hangs over us like some vast umbrella,
shading us from all the world's banes and ills.
            Come,
                we raise our glasses to you
                our summer lady,
                our gentle aristocrat
                our friend.

Whiteness

In this cruel light, where the loathsome white drips through
the conduit, I cannot see to see.
I long for the soft shades of black, and if my wounds do not
soon destroy me, the white shall.

> I have been floundering, floundering in this part of
> the pipe for hours.
> Yet I dare not call out for help, even though my
> body
> is bleeding furiously,
> for I fear those above and below.
> Great chunks of my flesh have been torn from my
> side,
> for the sleek members of my tribe were jubilant
> when
> they attacked and made a pretty thorough job of
> me with
> their sharp teeth.
> I am weakening, weakening as I feel my own life's
> blood draining away . . .
> But this is not quite so horrible as the ugly white
> that glares above me.

My beginnings were likely enough.
Long and lean but strong was my father,
and mother was fairly tall.
But I never grew to any considerable size,
so when I entered the group, I did not fight for dominance.
The others were too stout and strong.
Yet though I was not overly big, I could render the tribe
certain services.
I could sense certain dangers and alert the community when it
was threatened . . . In time they came to value me, and when
I took a mate, there
was no fighting to get her.

In those days, we lived near great stores of food
thrown extravagantly about in alleys or stored in
great masses in warehouses.
We thrived happily, for we were then few and
provisions were many.
But soon we grew to a larger and larger
    community.
We became so many that frequently there were
    fights
over females and food.
But despite these troubles, we lived on.

But one day those who lived on the pavements above us
grew to enormous numbers, and their food became scarcer
and scarcer.
Soon nothing was left for us in the warehouses and alleys,
and frequently there were mass hunts to ferret us out for
    food.

Our own provisions soon dwindled almost to nothing.
Larger members began chasing smaller ones away,
and the females were snatched away from the weakest.
For a while, they allowed me to keep my mate,
but today, several attacked me viciously.
In a short time, they had gnashed and torn my flesh
and whisked my wife away.
I fled bleeding to this conduit,
and now I await whatever comes.

Stories of our tribe go back to a time,
so long ago that we have forgotten dates:
when my people lived upon the earth
rather than beneath it
and fed on twigs and leaves.
But one day we went underground.
It seems to me that this move
was most unnatural;
somewhere, we did go wrong.

Somehow, this dying seems unimportant;
it was always puzzling to be alive.
Since I dare not hunt for food in the light above
and dare not go back to the nest,
there is nothing left for me to do.
I am hungry and hurting and the light above me
torments me.
And soon, very soon, I shall die.

Lines to H.S.F.

At first . . . with your peg-leg mind and your peep-hole soul
        bursting to the surface
                        of thin, multi-veined networks
                        of blood (high) and intellect
                        ("so and so")

one thinks of a "pop-up" from a Godey's Lady Book (if there
    had been one).

                Once Sebastian painted a portrait of
                you, posed seriously before your Victorian
                stairwell, like some *pukka sahib*, once
                exultant in Burma, but now shabby-genteel.

Yet there are others   stirring   within you.

One could be flip and say there is a decayed fineness that has
    more energy and —
               and more authority than the best in others like
                    myself
              who are topheavy with dullness.

But this misses the mark,
                    misses despite the fact that one
                        forever thinks
                    of some fawning courtier —
                        obsequious, simpering, politic —
                in the court of some effete king.

Forgetting that there is more effeteness in the
muscles of football players or in the faked piled-up
wigs of street women than in a pinch of you.

For nowhere in you is the role faked:
when joking airily with the paper boy
or talking earnestly with the next-door neighbor
or chatting about certain popular but ridiculous celebrities
who are your substitute for some faded aristocracy.

all these — somehow — pass muster.

For your anchorage is rooted deep in some sense of human
        worth,
in the belief that without affection — not love. not that —
without deep and heartfelt affection
life is seriously and fatally damaged.

Beneath, then,
                the windmill chatter, the ritualized drinking
                    (where tippling
                becomes as ceremonious as the taking of snuff
                    by some
                powdered and beauty-spotted eighteenth
                    century earl)

there emerges our own Mr. Micawber — hurrying from drink
                                    to drink;
                                    without
                                    stumbling,
                                without ill temper.
                                Delighting in
                                everyone and
                                everything you meet.
Somehow . . . anyhow . . . . it all works true.

60

Kent State, 1970

— To My Students in Their Profound Sadness

I.

This is the worst of all possible times;
the hours are bleak and unbearable;
all. all seems intolerable.
It is dark. dark everywhere
but darkest most in your hurt young eyes.
We have snatched your green years
gagged all those shouts of joy,
leaving only your baffled silence.
I watch as you sit before me;
you cannot write a note,
cannot read a page.
My mind reaches out to find some word, some ploy.
that will help all that brooding pain;
but my lips utter the empty phrase:
I cannot salve that hurt.

II.

I sit at the old desk
the shaken *doyen*, whose old bag of platitudes leaks trash.
There is no making of a vineyard from a curse:
optimism does not stem from deepest terror:
our glittering eyes are not gay.
I have trafficked in lies.

III.

We have hacked and hacked
and now the corpus of the age
lies stinking before you.
We stand, then, condemned before you,
bleeding, bloated felons.
Yet our feet keep thrashing. thrashing,
and our lips keep moving, moving,
reaching, ever reaching. for another
crooked phrase.

Biography

Al Montesi was born in Memphis, Tennessee, of immigrant Italian parents who had come to the American South from Ancona, Italy, during the 1890's. He was brought up in the South during the beginnings of the "Southern Renaissance" when William Faulkner was writing out of Oxford, Mississippi, and the Fugitive-Agrarians were installed at Vanderbilt. Schooling in Memphis (CBC, a Christian Brothers' High School) and then from 1941-1943 a stint in the Army Air Corps as a control tower operator. After the War, schooling at the University of Tennessee, Northwestern (B.S.), University of Michigan (M.A.), a year with Alan Swallow at the University of Denver, and then a Ph.D. at Pennsylvania State University. He has taught at The Citadel, Penn State, SUNY at Buffalo, N.Y., Wesleyan University (Middletown, Conn.), The University of the Ruhr (Bochum, Germany), and at St. Louis University where he has been assistant, associate, and full professor over a period of almost twenty years. Editor (*Talisman, Twentieth Century Literature*), lecturer ("James Joyce" at Trinity University, Dublin), critic and poet (*Micrograms*, Maryhurst Press, 1971), Montesi has taught creative writing at SLU during his stay in St. Louis.